Hillary Clinton

Remarkable American Politician

by Dan Kinney

Abdo
HISTORY MAKER
BIOGRAPHIES
Kids

abdopublishing.com

Published by Abdo Kids, a division of ABDO, PO Box 398166, Minneapolis, Minnesota 55439.

Copyright © 2018 by Abdo Consulting Group, Inc. International copyrights reserved in all countries. No part of this book may be reproduced in any form without written permission from the publisher.

Printed in the United States of America, North Mankato, Minnesota.

102017

012018

Photo Credits: AP Images, Getty Images, Granger Collection, Shutterstock, ©Joseph Sohm p.Cover / Shutterstock.com

Production Contributors: Teddy Borth, Jennie Forsberg, Grace Hansen

Design Contributors: Laura Mitchell, Dorothy Toth

Publisher's Cataloging-in-Publication Data

Names: Kinney, Dan, author.

Title: Hillary Clinton: remarkable American politician / by Dan Kinney.

Other titles: Remarkable American politician

Description: Minneapolis, Minnesota : Abdo Kids, 2018. | Series: History maker biographies |
     Includes glossary, index and online resource (page 24).

Identifiers: LCCN 2017943147 | ISBN 9781532104268 (lib.bdg.) | ISBN 9781532105388 (ebook) |
     ISBN 9781532105944 (Read-to-me ebook)

Subjects: LCSH: Clinton, Hillary Rodham, 1947- --Juvenile literature. | United States--Congress--Senate
     --Biography--Juvenile literature. | United States--Congress--Senate--Juvenile literature.

Classification: DDC 973.929 [B]--dc23

LC record available at https://lccn.loc.gov/2017943147

Table of Contents

Early Years

Hillary Diane Rodham was born on October 26, 1947. She grew up in Park Ridge, Illinois.

Illinois

In high school, Hillary was

in the **student government**.

She won the award "Most Likely

to Succeed." She graduated in

the top 5 percent of her class.

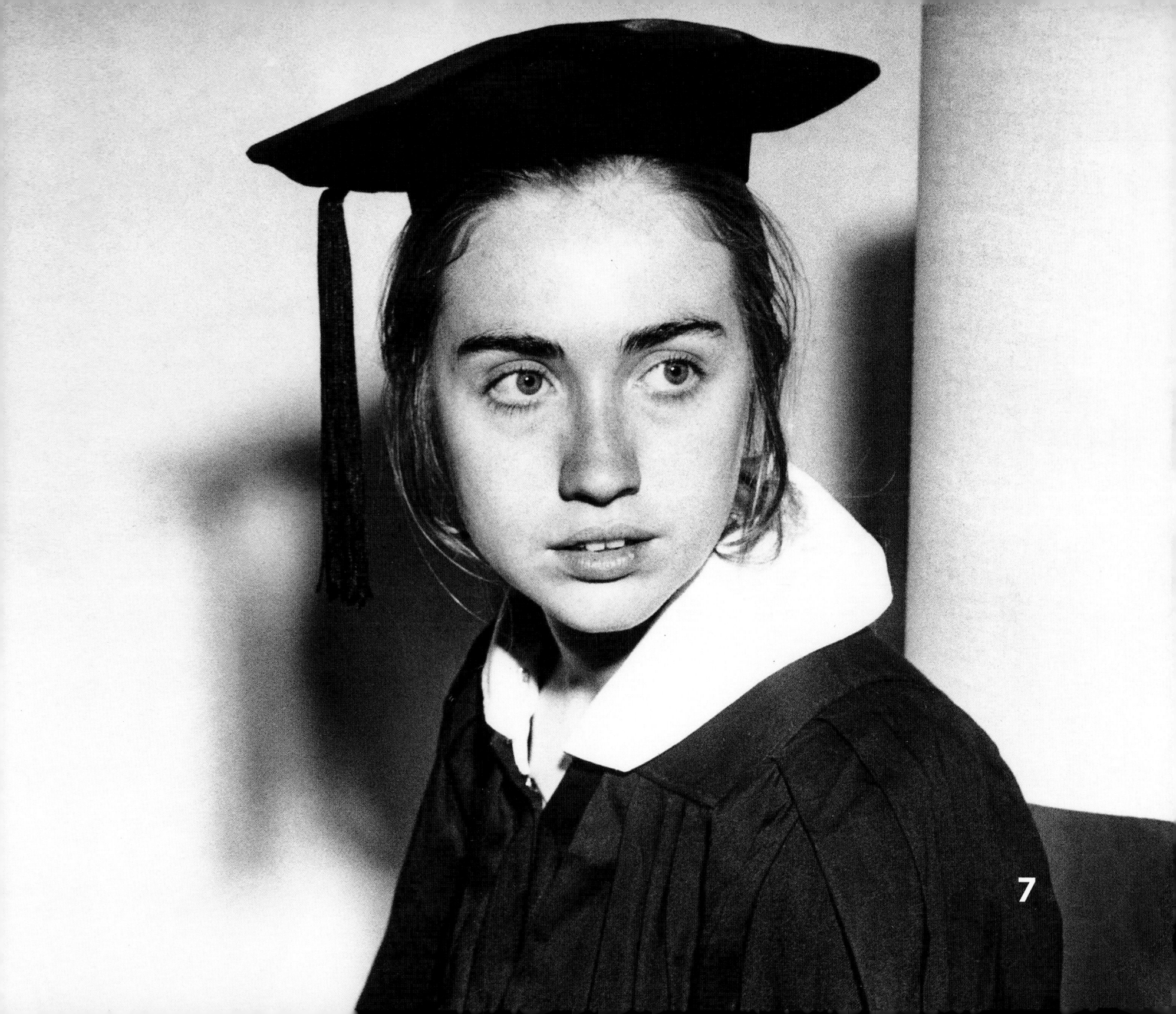
7

Higher Education

Hillary attended Wellesley

College. There she found a

passion for helping people.

Hillary went on to attend Yale Law School. There she met her husband, future US president Bill Clinton. After law school, the two moved to Fayetteville, Arkansas.

11

Bill became governor of Arkansas in 1979. Hillary served as First Lady. She worked hard to help the state's poorest areas. She gave birth to daughter Chelsea in 1980.

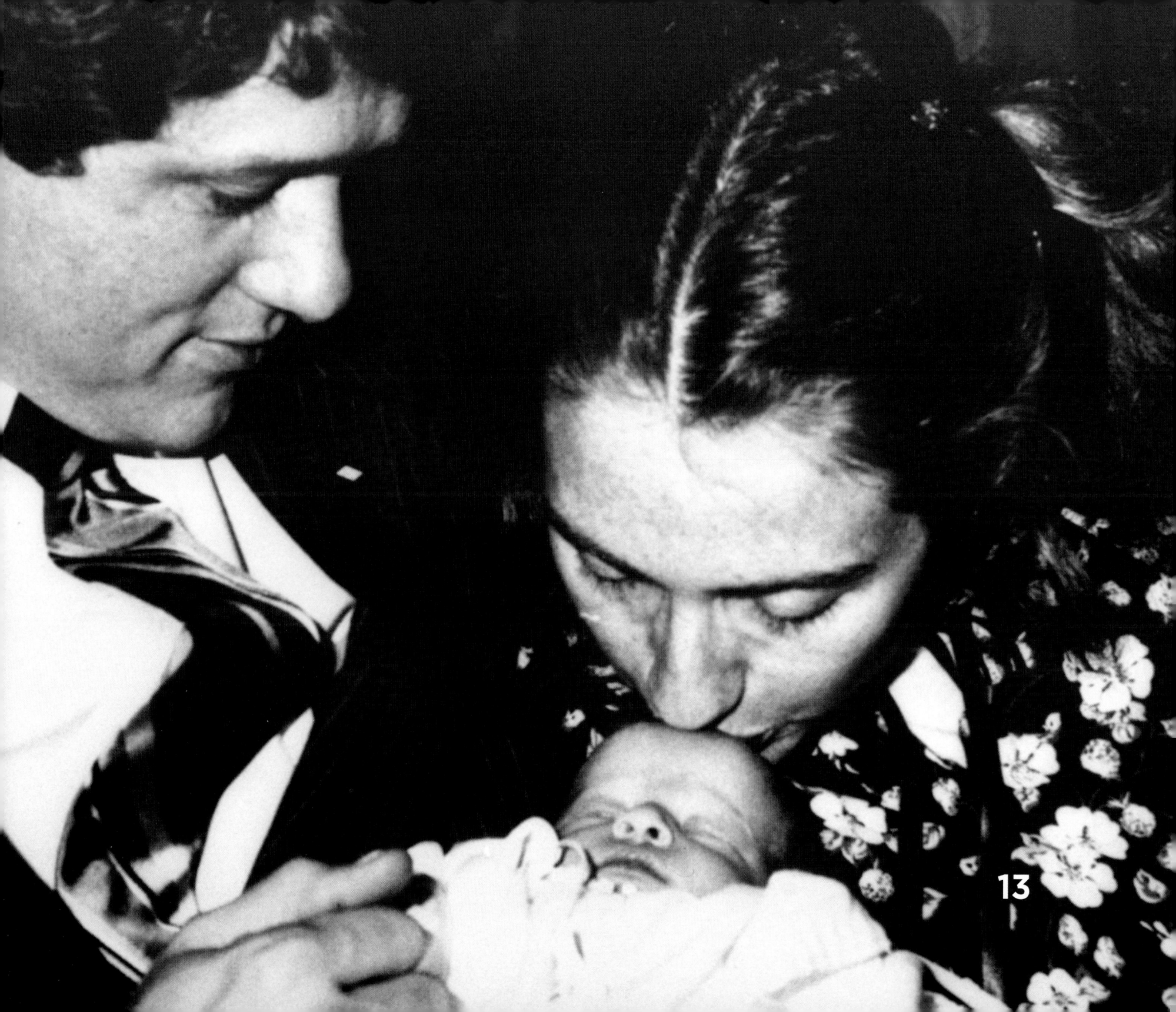

13

First Lady & Senator

In 1992, Bill was elected president of the United States. Hillary served as First Lady. In 2000, Hillary ran for **senator** of New York. She became the state's first female senator.

15

Running for President

In 2007, Hillary ran for president.

She lost to President Barack

Obama. But Obama chose

her to be **secretary of state**.

17

In 2015, Clinton ran for president a second time. She became the first female **nominee** of a major American **party**.

November 8, 2016, was a sad day for Hillary's supporters. She had lost the election. After she lost she said, "Let us not grow weary. . . for there is more work to do."

21

Timeline

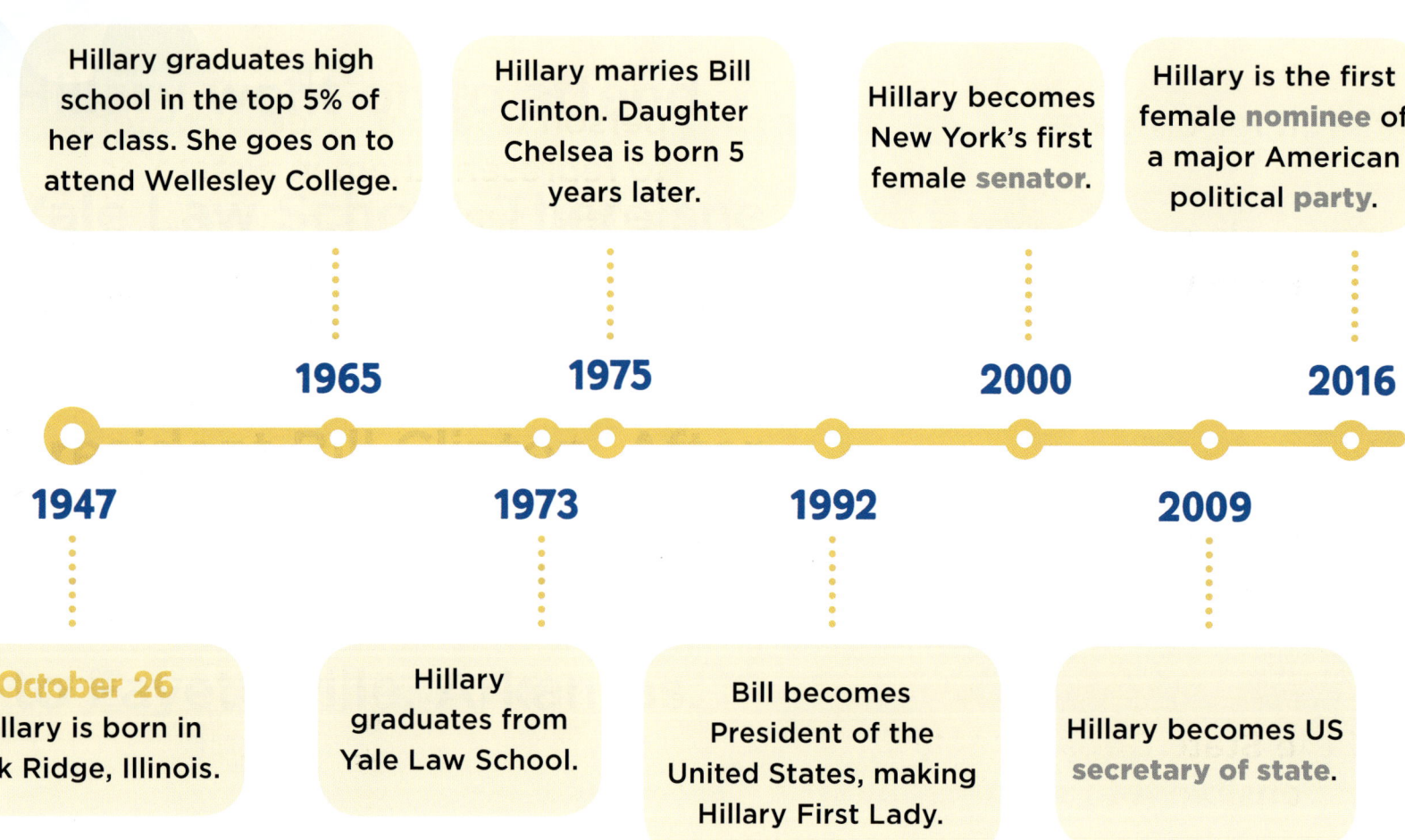

Hillary graduates high school in the top 5% of her class. She goes on to attend Wellesley College.

Hillary marries Bill Clinton. Daughter Chelsea is born 5 years later.

Hillary becomes New York's first female senator.

Hillary is the first female nominee of a major American political party.

1965   **1975**   **2000**   **2016**

1947   **1973**   **1992**   **2009**

October 26
Hillary is born in Park Ridge, Illinois.

Hillary graduates from Yale Law School.

Bill becomes President of the United States, making Hillary First Lady.

Hillary becomes US secretary of state.

Glossary

nominee – a person chosen to run for office.

party – in government, a group of people with similar political beliefs. The Republican Party and Democratic Party are examples.

passion – a strong feeling of enthusiasm and excitement for something.

secretary of state – the head of the State Department, responsible for foreign affairs.

senator – in government, a person who is elected by voters to represent them in a state or federal senate.

student government – a group of students who are elected to help plan and organize activities and events for other students.

Index

Abdo Kids ONLINE

FREE! ONLINE MULTIMEDIA RESOURCES

Visit **abdokids.com** and use this code to access crafts, games, videos, and more!

Abdo Kids Code:
HHK4268